T0209401

FROM
LEGACY TO
DYNASTY

FROM
LEGACY TO
DYNASTY

HOW TO
CREATE
GENERATIONAL
WEALTH

THE BUSINESS ACQUISITION BLUEPRINT

AFAM ELUE

FROM LEGACY TO DYNASTY
HOW TO CREATE GENERATIONAL WEALTH

THE BUSINESS ACQUISITION BLUEPRINT

iUniverse books may be ordered through booksellers or by contacting:

iUniverse
1663 Liberty Drive
Bloomington, IN 47403
www.iuniverse.com
844-349-9409

ISBN: 978-1-6632-5388-0 (sc)
ISBN: 978-1-6632-5390-3 (hc)
ISBN: 978-1-6632-5389-7 (e)

Library of Congress Control Number: 2023910998

Print information available on the last page.

iUniverse rev. date: 08/01/2023

CONTENTS

INTRODUCTION

We are right now, as you read this book entering one of the most lucrative opportunities in the history of the human race.

Fortunes will be made by those who see it. Generational wealth will be created, and opportunities to spread opportunity and wealth to people who've yet to experience are here.

The only question is this... are you going to be a part of it or left behind?

In the United States (and to a lesser degree in other countries) the Baby Boomers are retiring. Yes, you already know this, but the opportunity is in what many of them are leaving behind.

Businesses.

Many Boomers started and grew small and mid-sized businesses. Now, they're looking to sell. They need to sell.

The business they've built is a major funding source for their retirement.

As a result, we're seeing an avalanche of businesses for sale in the United States.

Most will never sell. Many will sell for pennies on the dollar.

And some savvy businesspeople will pickup bargain businesses and turn them into profit machines.

This book is about doing just that.

I have written it for three types of people:

The first is the entrepreneur who has a business and is looking to exit soon. I will show you how to approach the exit to maximize the value of your business.

The second is the investor who wants to capitalize on this massive opportunity to create outsized returns with relatively low risk.

The third is the integrator who is skilled at operating and growing a business but might lack the capital to invest—I'll show you how to partner with investors, create cash and equity and build real wealth for yourself.

......

It is widely believed that the top three priorities for the average person are:

1. Your health
2. Your relationships
3. Your wealth

Your health could include physical, mental, emotional, or even spiritual health.

Your relationships typically involve friends and family. But could also include professional as well as personal relationships.

Lastly, your wealth is self explanatory. It could be argued that, by addressing your wealth status, the probability of ending up with better health and better relationships, is much higher.

Most Americans say that to be considered "wealthy" in the U.S. in 2021, you need to have a net worth of **nearly $2 million** — $1.9 million to be exact.

According to Schwab's 2021 Modern Wealth Survey, wealth expectations also varied by generation, with younger Americans saying they felt that lower net worth could be considered wealthy.

Here's the net worth each generation says you need to be considered wealthy in 2021:

- Millennials (ages 24 to 39): $1.4 million
- Gen X (ages 44 to 55): $1.9 million
- Baby boomers (ages 56 to 74): $2.5 million

The drop in the net worth expectations could be due to the Covid-19 pandemic. Over half of 1,000 survey respondents, reported that they were financially impacted in some way by the pandemic.

A drop in income can impact net worth, which is essentially a calculation of all of a person's assets — including cash in checking and savings accounts, financial investments and the value of any real estate or vehicles owned — minus all their debt, including credit card balances, student loans and mortgages.

Still, even before the pandemic affected employment, most Americans had nowhere near a net worth of $1.9 million.

Regardless of how your own net worth changed over the past year, it's likely worth taking the time to evaluate where you're at right now and starting to plan, for the future.

This book will unpack the topic of generational wealth creation and preservation, through the mechanism of business acquisitions.

Generational wealth creation (and preservation) is a trending topic in today's popular culture.

Especially with a backdrop to:

1. Baby Boomers/ Approaching retirement.
2. The Great Resignation
3. Equity, Diversity, and Inclusion (EDI)

BABY BOOMERS

The Challenge with Baby Boomers approaching retirement includes:

- Majority owners of SME (small & medium sized enterprise) businesses are baby boomers. Which means that when they retire there will be a service gap in the marketplace for the value, they provide in those communities
- No Succession planning/Legacy. This means that cultivating the right successor to carry on the business and preserve the good reputation of the business, is crucial.
- Need for Nest Egg/Wealth Preservation. If the business owner is unable to maintain their current lifestyle once that income goes away when they retire, that is a problem.

THE GREAT RESIGNATION

The great resignation is this new phenomenon where professionals who are dissatisfied with current work-life balance, glass ceilings and unfulfillment, are looking to other alternatives than the regular 9-5.

Symptoms of this trend include:

- Corporate Loyalty on the Decline
- Entrepreneurship on the Rise
- Business acquisition as the fastest means to create wealth

EDI (EQUITY-DIVERSITY-INCLUSION)

This is hot topic in today's public awareness.

However, it is also a sensitive subject, especially when there are more questions than answers, more problem statements than solution offerings.

In this book, we are proposing an economic solution for EDI.

We are suggesting that the *healing* sought by equity seeking groups can start with the wealth conversation in terms of *healing your wallet.*

We propose acquisition entrepreneurship as the mechanism to level the playing field.

Imagine a world where those with an entrepreneurial or growth mindset can accumulate assets through business acquisitions as a vehicle for creating wealth.

Imagine how much business opportunity or job safety you would be creating for those less inclined towards entrepreneurship.

How good will it feel to not only own profitable businesses and keep people employed, but to also to preserve your wealth and legacy, for generations to come?

Now if there was a way to be guided towards the Creation and Preservation of wealth, without any hassle or missteps- would you take it?

Wealth generally refers to the abundance of valuable resources or assets that an individual, organization, or nation possesses.

These resources or assets can include money, property, investments, natural resources, intellectual property, and other valuable possessions.

Wealth is often measured in terms of financial value and can be accumulated through various means such as inheritance, entrepreneurship, investment, or employment.

However, wealth can also be subjective and can include factors such as social status, power, and influence. Different people may have different definitions of wealth depending on their cultural, social, and economic backgrounds.

Although our subject matter is focused on the creation and preservation of wealth, there is much more to gain than just the monetary value.

There is also freedom of time associated with owning a business.

Some work in-the-business, others work on-the business, you as the owner will work above-the-business.

This provides you time freedom and could allow you to own multiple businesses if you choose.

The freedom, not just to pay for your lifestyle, but also to explore other passions that you may have or want to cultivate.

Now on the opposite end of the spectrum, what is at stake if we fail to act, is security. Financial security. Emotional security. And so on.

If your status quo is to work for a paycheck, then consider the question of long-term job security.

If your status quo is to start a business, then think about the statistics of how many start ups fail in the first 5 years.

If your status quo is to invest in alternatives like the stock market or real estate, then be ready for major FOMO (fear of missing out), when you learn that you have been leaving money on the table.

CHAPTER 1

The most important new investment opportunity of the 21st Century

The reason why this topic is important is for three main reasons.

One, the *baby boomer* generation is retiring at record numbers.

Two, the *great resignation*. This is where corporate loyalty is on a decline. Entrepreneurship is on the rise. And people are realizing that business acquisition is the fastest means to creating wealth.

Three, the idea of equity, diversity, and inclusion, also known as EDI.

This is where we talk about living and working in a *Just Society*.

Here we identify the three core pillars of any society as including: security, culture, and economics.

So, the first point about baby boomers, the greatest transfer of wealth is happening right now, and is being driven at least in part, by the movement of inheritance from one generation to another. Yet, as millions of baby boomers are actively passing along their savings to their children, one thing is at risk of being left behind the business they own. Baby Boomers defined as people born between the years of 1946 and 1964, accounted for approximately 40% of small businesses or franchise ownership in the world.

Many of these are service based businesses, restaurants, auto shops, plumbing businesses, local retail stores, hardware repair companies and more. With that in mind, consider this. Experts estimate that roughly 10,000 baby boomers retire each day. Yes, read that right each day. However, early indicators show that the logical inheritors of these businesses may not be interested in taking over the reins. This puts the future of many small businesses in question.

Millennials have a wider array of career choices that never existed for their parents and instead have also demonstrated a desire for more flexibility and independence. A report from smart assets illustrates that large numbers of this generation are gravitating towards jobs and technology, healthcare, media, and operations.

Gen Z is not too far off, according to a report from Glassdoor a meaningful portion of Gen Z is most interested in working in the tech sector. Collectively, these data points represent a future where the likely successor of these baby boomer owned businesses may not want to take over the family business.

Think about your neighbor who successfully grew a local restaurant franchise from one location to multiple stores, or that family or retail store that you visit every few months. These proprietors have built companies with strong local brands, real revenue, and loyal customers. What is next for their business when they retire?

What may be most surprising is that three fourths of baby boomers' own businesses are profitable. According to statistics from guided financial. The baby boomer generation accounts for an estimated 2.3 million small businesses in the United States, which cumulatively employ over 25 million people.

Many these businesses are thriving and nearly 60% have no succession or transition plan in place. Are we nearing a breaking point where the supply of successful small businesses will outpace the demand of ownership for them? Let's hope not. If someone doesn't seize on these businesses, we all could be sitting around in 10 years with fewer plumbers available to fix your toilet and nothing but chain restaurants serving newborn meals.

The next point for why this topic is important, has to do with the great resignation. The great resignation, also known as the Big quit, and the great reshuffle is an ongoing economic trend in which employees have voluntarily resigned from their jobs and mass beginning early 2021.

Possible causes include wage stagnation, amid rising cost of living, long lasting job of dissatisfaction, safety concerns of the COVID 19 pandemic, and a desire to work for companies with better remote working policies. Some economists have described the great resignation as akin to a general strike. The term great resignation was coined by Anthony Klotz, a Professor of Management at University College London School of Management in May 2001, when he predicted a sustained mass exodus.

The COVID 19 pandemic set of nearly unprecedented churn in the US labor market, widespread job losses in the early months of the pandemic gave way too tight labor markets in 2021, driven in part by what's come to be known as the great resignation, the measures quit rates reached a 20-year high last November.

A new Pew Research Center survey finds that low pay and lack of opportunity for advancement and feeling disrespected at work are the top reasons why Americans quit their jobs last year. The survey also finds that those who quit and are now employed elsewhere. More likely than not to see their current job has better pay more opportunities for advancement, and more work life balance and flexibility.

And even higher percentages of those within the great resignation group seeking entrepreneurship opportunities to create their own destinies work like life balance, and wealth creation for themselves and generations to come.

The last point on this topic of wealth creation and preservation is the topic of EDI, which stands for equity, diversity, and inclusion.

Here we address the ideal *just society*.

We use the term society loosely, to describe any organization of people, ranging from a business organization to the community at large.

If the core pillars of society would include items such as: security, culture, and economics, then what would wealth distribution in an EDI conscious society look like?

Security could be physical or cybersecurity.

Culture equates to sustainability.

And Economics means prosperity in terms of equity.

And what is an equitable or inclusive distribution of wealth? What would that look like?

Here we are going to talk about wealth creation, within the context of Equity, Diversity, and Inclusion and as it pertains to entrepreneurship.

Minority or racialized groups would typically talk about the glass ceiling in the corporate environment or systemic issues that preclude their economic advantage.

The problem is a lack of cultural awareness and acceptance.

The challenge is that you cannot legislate emotional acceptance or human perceptions.

The solution is for these groups to leverage every goodwill available to them, to create ecosystems through entrepreneurship that will level the playing field and provide unlimited opportunities for financial and time freedom, and respect.

CHAPTER 2

Why Investors, Entrepreneurs, and Integrators Need Each Other Now

In this chapter, I want to introduce the main actors of an M&A (merger and acquisition) transaction within our model. There are three characters involved, namely: the Investor, the Integrator, and the Entrepreneur.

Let us take a look at them one by one.

The investor.

Who is an investor?

We define an investor here as anyone with disposable cash to invest or has access to investable funds.

The term investor in our environment is defined loosely to include anyone from a *search funder* to a *fund manager*.

A Search Funder is someone who looks for deals, preferably off market deals, through several channels.

May be through referrals, marketing efforts, or other different kinds of outreach.

Then once they find a deal which meets their investment criteria, they must determine if the business owner is a motivated seller.

A motivated seller is someone that typically has a pressing reason why they must sell their business.

Reasons such as need for cash in or cash out; shiny object syndrome; divorce; health; partner dispute; retirement; upcycle or down cycle; relocation; death; or burn out.

Once identified, the search funder gets them under a *letter of intent*, which is essentially a proposal for the price and terms to complete the sale of the business.

Then they proceed to look for funding sources to acquire the business.

So as a Search Funder, they **search** and then they **fund** a deal.

On the other hand, you have a fund manager. This is someone who sits on a pool of funds to be deployed into viable investments.

The funds could be institutional money or from a group of investors or just family money.

A fund manager is also looking for deals, preferably off market deals, and they have an investment criterion, whether it is by size, in terms of revenue, profitability, staff strength, and or quality, in terms of industry, sector, and so on.

These fund managers would use those criteria to find deals and have the funds to acquire those companies promptly. So that is also considered an investor.

The next category to describe is the integrator. Now, the integrator is an M&A intermediary. What we mean by that is, these are people that are either involved in the marketing and sales side of M&A, the operation side, or the finance side.

They could be a financial intermediary that helps to provide deal financing options like loans or equity investors.

They could be a marketing agency operating in the media space- to drive awareness and generate leads.

They could be an operation intermediary, which means that the people that make things happen. These are the people that see to the day-to-day workings of a company.

So, these are intermediaries and called integrators in this context. They are the people that help with exit strategies, with expansion of companies and efficient management of companies.

Now, what does the integrator want?

The integrator wants to be an investor.

They want to invest sweat equity.

To have participation in the upside of the value that they help create -when they grow and scale a company.

The integrator necessarily wants to have profit interest.

So, let us recap. The integrator is someone who makes businesses grow and scale exponentially. And what they want is to participate in the value that they create for businesses.

Now, who is an integrator?

This could be anyone from a self-employed professional, freelancer, consultant, any of those kinds of titles, all the way to an agency.

They could be a solo operator that is operating as a self-employed freelancer, contractor or somewhere in between as a consultant.

Or a boutique agency that helps to accelerate businesses, either through marketing and sales to operational efficiency, or through financial intermediation.

That is an integrator.

Finally, we talk about the entrepreneur.

The entrepreneur in our model is defined as anyone from a *wantrepreneur* to a business owner.

A *wantrepreneur* is a person who is intending to take the risk required to own a business but have not quite taken the leap or figured things out yet.

They have not made the complete transition from a side hustle or 9 to 5, into running a business as a full-time endeavor.

They desire to create a product or service and answer to nobody but themselves, and basically become their own boss.

So that is a *wantrepreneur*.

Then, on the opposite end of the spectrum is the business owner.

This is somebody who operates above the business.

They run the business; the business does not run them.

They have figured things out. Systems, Product-Market fit, Staffing, and so on.

They offer a product or service and have an established client base.

They have revenue and might even be profitable.

And they have been through business cycles and existed for a significant period of time.

That is the business owner.

So, anyone in this space between *wantrepreneur* and business owner is who we are categorizing as the entrepreneur.

What does the entrepreneur want?

They want growth, they want expansion, whether it be local or international, and they want to scale their business exponentially.

They want an exit at some point, which could be a major liquidity event.

After which, in some cases, the entrepreneur could be open to the option to continue to serve the business and its customers, potentially as a consultant to the business.

This means that the entrepreneur sells his business and gets their exit package, then may want to be retained part time as advisor or consultant to the business- now working reduced hours, and only focused on doing what they love within the business.

This is the ideal exit scenario for a typical entrepreneur.

Our work is to bring these three characters together in a cohesive way that makes for a deal to be done, ongoing operations to be managed, and the prospect of wealth creation greatly optimized for all involved.

Compare this approach to traditional M&A (mergers and acquisitions) deals where success rates can vary widely depending on various factors such as industry, deal size, and the specific circumstances of each transaction. Studies have shown that a significant percentage of M&A deals fail to achieve their intended outcomes.

According to a study by McKinsey & Company, approximately 70% of M&A deals do not achieve their intended value creation objectives. Another study by Harvard Business Review found that the failure rate of M&A deals ranges from 70% to 90%, depending on the deal size.

There are several reasons why M&A deals can fail to achieve their intended outcomes. The most common reasons include lack of strategic fit, poor due diligence, and poor post-merger integration.

A lack of strategic fit between the two companies. In other words, the companies may not have compatible cultures, business models, or goals, which can make it difficult to integrate the two organizations effectively.

The other factor that can contribute to M&A failure is poor due diligence. If the acquiring company fails to thoroughly assess the target company's financial, legal, and operational risks and opportunities, it can lead to unexpected challenges and costs down the line.

Additionally, issues with post-merger integration can also contribute to a high failure rate. Even if the two companies are a good strategic fit, integrating their operations, systems, and cultures can be a complex and challenging process. If the integration is not managed effectively, it can lead to employee disengagement, customer dissatisfaction, and other problems that can undermine the success of the deal.

By using our model, where the buyer (investor), operator (integrator) and seller (entrepreneur) are all involved in the deal making process from the onset, most of the issues that cause failure can be mitigated.

CHAPTER 3

Why Start-ups suck!

Statistics show that start-ups have a 90% failure rate.10% fail in the first year and 70% fail between year 2 and 5.Some of the reasons for this include:-No market demand-First time founder-Not the right team-Run out of money......and so on. You get the idea!A safer alternative is to buy an existing business.With the Baby-Boomer generation retiring at record numbers, the opportunity for acquisitions is endless.Here a few good reasons to consider buying vs to build a business from scratch: 1. Less Risk 2. Better Financing Options 3.Brand Recognition 4. Instant Customers 5. Instant Sales 6. Instant Profits 7. Instant Contacts 8. Instant Systems 9. Instant Employees

In this chapter, we want to talk about what is a stake for the investor, for the integrator and for the entrepreneur.

So, we'll take the investor first, what is a stake for the investor for not acting on the opportunity to acquire businesses to create wealth? There will be three elements to be discussed in this context. One is FOMO. FOMO stands for fear of missing out.

The next is ROI, which stands for return on investments. And the third point is principal risk. So, let us take FOMO first, the investor ultimately wants to be in on the ground floor, where they can invest in something at a lower price and exit at a higher price.

So, the rule of investing 101 is to buy low, and sell high. And there is a constant fear of missing out when opportunities come that are well valued, well priced. And you do not want to miss out on those opportunities. So therein lies FOMO.

Therefore, the risk of not acting quickly, or even thinking about how to prepare for an acquisition transaction is the risk of FOMO where you could miss out if you are not well positioned to take advantage of market opportunities.

The second investor risk is ROI.

This is for return on investment. Investors know about investing in real estate, they know about investing in the stock market. But investing in business acquisition, for small to medium enterprises, is something that is largely unknown in the marketplace, to the average investor.

However, if you compare the different modalities of investments, the return on investment with business acquisition is exponentially higher in the private equity space, exponentially higher.

With the stock market and real estate investments, you could get five to 7% year over year return and feel like you have done well for yourself.

Then, on the high end of the stock markets 10,11 or 12% returns and fund managers are singing their own praises. But in the private equity space, when you acquire a business, the exponential return is limitless.

You could have 2x, 3x, or 10x return on your investments in short order by pulling certain drivers such as Sales and Marketing, Financial and Operational efficiencies, which will ultimately improve the bottom line and produce a higher return on investment for the investor.

So, the ROI is at stake if an investor is not well positioned to acquire businesses or to take advantage of the opportunity currently in the marketplace.

And the final point for the investor is principal risk. This is the mitigation of loss of capital. So, here when you acquire a business, you acquire it as an asset.

So that business becomes a tangible property for you as an investor, right. Whether it is a physical asset like the business property or a piece of equipment, or it could be intellectual property like your goodwill or client list, the team you have in place, all these things are assets, that are -in the worst-case scenario-able to mitigate the risk of losing your entire capital.

Therefore, the principal risk, in my opinion is substantially lower in the private equity space than anywhere else.

The next category is what is at stake for the integrator. There are three items here to discuss. One is the *dancing bear syndrome*. Okay.

The next is *always the bridesmaid*, never the bride. And the last one is *Seat at the table*.

So, the first one is the dancing bear syndrome is where the integrator is at risk of their high-ticket income stopping when their performance stops. This is the risk of being a high value integrator that is always delivering value through performance. But that income stops once you stop delivering.

That is a great risk. So, for those integrators who have been in business 20-30 years, that still must put on a show, still must do events, still must train people at a very high level to attract the kind of income that they are accustomed to. That is the dancing bear trap.

And then always the bridesmaid never the bride. This is where you have helped people as an integrator to build their empires, okay. You have come in, and you've poured gasoline on the fire and made businesses grow and accelerated, you know how to make the business scale, and you get a salary, and a bonus, you get income, but not equity in the growth that you've helped to create.

That is basically being "always the bridesmaid never the bride". And that is a risk of an integrator, of not getting into the business acquisition mindset.

Seat at the table. This is where it is time to be owners of capital, and not just managers.

An integrator is typically a professional that has high value skills in management, in growth architecture, in, strategic influence, or financial expertise. But they are not the owners of the capital. Okay, they are operators.

And that leads to discontentment over time, where they feel like they are not getting their place, or they are due recognition for the value that they bring to this entire ecosystem. And the third party to this chapter of what is at stake is the entrepreneur.

Here, there are three things to consider, as a state for the entrepreneur, they can keep working longer than they want to, to, they can accept and unwilling or incompetent kids or employees as their successor.

Or the third option is to close the business and live off a reverse mortgage in their retirement.

Option one: keep working longer than you want to.

So, an entrepreneur has a business, and they have clients to serve, they have a good product, and they're getting up there in age and determined that they should be able to exit at some point, they should be able to slow down their productivity at some point, or even leave all together to do something else. Maybe focus on some hobbies or to, you know, pursue other passions, with the energy and time they have left.

But that is hardly ever the case when they are tied to their business with no potential successor on the horizon. So, they end up working longer than they must.

I met a gentleman yesterday in the IT space who told me he was 90 years old. 90 years old. That is a long time to still be doing IT implementations. And, you know, once the subject of an exit, or a retirement package came up, everything changed. Light bulbs went on.

He was interested to learn more about how it would work.

It piqued his interest.

So, if that was the first time, he had heard about it, this tells me that there are many entrepreneurs out there that are subject, okay, not forced, but subject to keep working longer than they have to, simply because they are unaware that they have options.

Option two: accept your unwilling or incompetent kids, or employees as your replacement to the run the business.

This is very risky situation because you build up a legacy of quality customer service, of good products, because of your duty of care.

Only to figure out that, in handing-off the business to your kids or employees to take over, that the quality of service will fall, if they do not have the same passion or vision as you do.

That is a big risk.

Option three: to close-down the business.

So once the entrepreneur is ready to leave for good, they just put up a *closing* sign and, you know, shut down the business and, you know, turn the lights off and essentially live off whatever they have saved up as their retirement nest egg, which in most cases is underfunded.

Or some people determine that their primary residence is an asset that they can live off. They want to do a reverse mortgage and pull all the equity out of the house and live on that. And you know, those in my humble opinion, are sub optimal solutions.

So that is what is at stake for the investor, the integrator, and the entrepreneur. For the investor it is FOMO, ROI (return on investment) and Principal Risk. For the integrator it is *dancing bear syndrome, always the bride number the bridesmaid* and missing the *seat at the table.*

And for the entrepreneur to *keep working longer than they have to, accept on willing successors* or *close down the business* and live off a reverse mortgage.

CHAPTER 4

Everything is timing

In this chapter, we want to talk about when is the time to act.

For the investor, we are positioning their primary objective as wealth creation.

For the integrator, the issue is the great resignation, which is happening across the US and across North America. And in some cases, all over the world.

For the entrepreneur, it is a legacy topic.

So, let us talk about the optimal timetables.

For the investor, the time to act is now- because in the previous chapter, we discussed FOMO (fear of missing out), which means that good deals do not wait.

The next item is time value of money. Which means that the sooner you start, the sooner you create your desired wealth.

Then finally, finding the right deal and the right deal team.

Finding the right team takes time. So, you must start now.

To recap, these are the three points for why acting now for the investor is vital:

1. Fear Of Missing Out, which means good deals do not wait.
2. Time value of money, which means that the longer you hold on to money, the more depreciated it gets.
3. And finding the right deal at the right time takes time, which is something you must cultivate over time, (at least 90 days).

Therefore, starting now gives you that runway to make that happen.

That is the case we make for acting Now; for the investor who wants to create wealth.

For the integrator, who is subject to the great resignation, where most of these high-level professionals are losing faith in the corporate agenda to be loyal to a company for a lifetime of service, and then get this retirement package that allows you to sail off into the sunset.

This is not the case anymore. High level professionals are finding that those retirement packages, or retirement savings programs are not as well funded as they used to be. And they are not guaranteed.

So, the integrator is losing their sense of loyalty to corporate America and figuring out that they must make their destiny for themselves.

Therefore, for the integrator we caution that "where your focus goes, your energy flows".

If you are giving your energy to corporate life, to an employer, that is your entire life, that is your focus. It is very difficult to have a divided focus and be productive at the same time.

So, the integrator must decide when to act in terms of moving their attention and their energy towards independently creating their own financial destiny.

The second point is there is no time like the present.

In putting this off and trying to move into entrepreneurship part time or waiting for an event to trigger that move into the investment or acquisition space, will always lead to further procrastination.

Therefore, the time to act as soon as you get the memo, that says you must create your own financial destiny, is now. No time like the present. And Time is money.

The idea of waiting for a future timetable, to start to create that wealth is also reducing the possibility of achieving your goals in time, for your retirement; in time for whatever milestones, you've set.

The best time to act on executing the plan to create wealth for yourself is now.

And then for entrepreneur whose focus is on legacy, they typically have a timeframe, if not right now- for an exit, it would be within a three-to-seven-year timeframe. Where the business needs to be prepared for sale at an optimal valuation.

The business needs to be packaged for an exit conversation.

So, within those three to seven years, there is a lot of preparation, a lot of work that goes into putting the marketing and sales processes in place or putting the operational processes and the documentation of those processes and for making the financial records stand up to any kind of due diligence.

So, all that work. Whether it is now or whether it is in three to seven years, needs to start now. Because at that time, it poses a headache, when you look back.

To assess what you have done in this timeframe for a potential acquirer or potential investor. It matters how much runway you have, with proper records.

The second point is that if you have concerns about what your legacy might be, you should start now. Okay, the culmination of your life's work in a package that is digestible, shareable, and unforgettable.

Which means that however you want to be remembered as a business that impacted your community, it is necessary to think of that today, rather than running around putting out fires, going round and around with transactions and responding to just what the day throws at you.

It is much more efficient, to start today to think about how you want to be remembered how you want to package that goodwill, whether it's in a book, whether it's in the business plan that you hand off to your successor, whether it's in the growth plan that someone else has to execute, to keep your legacy alive, all of that planning has to start now.

And then finally, if you want the wealth you created to outlive you and even your descendants, then the best time to find out how, is now.

So, it does take some work to understand the lifecycle of a merger and acquisition transaction.

To get in the headspace of an exit strategy or taking in an investment.

So as an entrepreneur the way to think about it is to begin the process of the research; to engage the professionals that will educate you along the way; that will introduce those elements that qualify your business for a higher valuation exit.

And, of course, the timing is always best to start-Now!

An example of timeframes is illustrated by the work we do for ABC (which stands for African Business Community). This is a social enterprise with the mission to create and preserve wealth for entrepreneurs of Afro-descent.

There is a thirteen-week course that provides an orientation for the acquisition entrepreneurship mindset and methodology. Followed by up to ten months to find and fund an acquisition deal. It would take another ninety days to a year to fully integrate the operations for stability and acceleration.

Knowing that your wealth acquisition strategy could be a one-to-two-year endeavour should provide you the sense of urgency to get started -now!

CHAPTER 5

L.I.F.T. D.A.D. – The strange sounding acronym that leads the way to Acquisition Success

In this chapter, we want to address how the mechanism works for accomplishing the prosperity outcomes described earlier.

For that, we have devised a success formula, we call L.I.F.T D-A-D for tactics and for strategy the acronym is L-E-G-S.

LIFT stands for:
Legal (L)
Insurance (I)
Finance (F), and
Tax (T)

DAD stands for:

Data (D)

Audience (A)

Dollars (D)

LEGS means (Leverage- Exit-Growth-Scale).

Here, we want to explore these different mechanisms might benefit our three unique personas: Investor-Integrator-Entrepreneur.

Starting first with the investor.

Now, the investor wants to get a deal done. What they typically need is contained in these four elements legal, insurance, finance, and tax, those are the big consideration for an investor.

So, a good team to have in place or a good infrastructure to have in place to serve the investor is to have legal advice, insurance protection, funding through financial intermediaries and then tax implications.

All of these must be addressed for the investor to feel complete in terms of doing an M&A transaction.

Now to the integrator, this is the D-A-D category.

The integrator is concerned with the deal facilitation.

That could involve marketing, operations, or finance activities.

What an integrator requires to be successful in this regard is D-A-D (data, audience, and dollars). So, the data could be typically a database, okay with several data points, whether that is a contact list or a CRM that already has existing information.

So, this data is what you can use to cultivate an audience. Or groups of people with common profiles or common problems. Groups that you can classify as target audience and create direct messaging that caters to them.

That was for audience.

Dollars -has to do with all of the monetary attributions that need to happen for value to exchange in this category.

Now whether that is the fee compensation for the integrator, or it's a revenue sharing arrangement with the business owner, or a profitability discussion, or some kind of equity release situation.

All of these come within the last D of dad, which is Dollars.

The third category is LEGS. L-E-G-S. Leverage, Exit growth and scale.

This is the focus for the entrepreneur because what they want to see is how to utilize what they currently have, like intellectual property or relationship capital -as leverage for an exit.

Once we have leverage, we want to create an exit, okay.

An exit does not have to be a permanent exit. It can be a partial exit.

It can be in terms of schedule. For instance, when you can exit a role in the company or occupy a position above the org chart, those are exits too. But the ultimate exit happens when you sell your company.

Whatever exit means to the entrepreneur, you can have our leverage to create an exit, and then integrate for growth and scale.

So that is the formula. That is the success formula.

That is the framework we have for these three categories, and for this entire ecosystem.

With this strategy, you get the benefit of a viable succession plan, along with a legacy of expansion, powered by a young talent- now so called : the angel investor.

A good way to describe how all these components might come together is to consider a real-life use case.

This example will include the three main actors in our framework, namely the investor, the integrator, and the entrepreneur.

For background, Jack is an absentee owner of a franchise pizza buffet restaurant in rural Arkansas. Due to a partner dispute, the restaurant has been losing money and requires a turnaround.

The owner is on the hook for a low interest SBA loan of four hundred and fifty thousand dollars. (SBA=small business administration)

The business makes over fifty thousand dollars a month in revenue but loses five thousand dollars after expenses and employee salaries are paid.

He needs someone familiar with the restaurant business to help run the day-to-day and manage costs and drive revenues.

At this point the owner just needs to break even and ensure that the SBA loan is being serviced and eventually paid off.

The problem is that hiring a typical manager won't cut it.

You end up with someone that applied to the job for a paycheck.

You will hardly get an entrepreneurial minded sales driver that will facilitate business development and strategic expansion initiatives.

Now Jack decides he wants to cut his loses and sell the business along with the debt. He starts to post the offer on social media sites and promote the deal.

However, time is ticking and there are no takers. The revenue is too low and the hint of debt and loses will scare off any investors or deal makers.

Fortunately, this M&A consultant discovers the situation and decides to help.

We introduce a resource that used to be a private chef, as the new investor. The investment will be sweat equity in exchange for 50% of the business.

Their objective will be to turn the business around within twelve months, by driving sales and manage operating costs.

After negotiations to iron out final details, the business purchase agreement is drawn up by the Legal team and executed by all parties involved.

Accountants also do a due diligence to ensure that the quality of earnings are accurate. They look at everything to do with the business insurance, financial statements, and tax returns.

Therefore, the deal is done with LIFT. (Legal-Insurance-Finance-Tax).

Then we for the DAD project. We draw up a business plan that gathers existing data, regarding revenue drivers, client acquisition costs and profitability margins.

We strategize on how to cultivate a captive audience that will account for stable sales numbers. Then we make dollar projections of six, twelve and thirty-six months for the budgetary input and bottom-line output for the business.

The final outcome is a win-win-win.

The sweat equity investor gets to own an asset and get paid along the way as the business grows.

Jack gets his SBA loan serviced and saved from the hassle of managing the day-to-day operations of the business. His minority equity will yield dividends as the profits grow and upon a sale of the business in three to five years, he will get twenty percent of the proceeds.

The dealmaker that puts this structure together keeps thirty percent profit only interest and offers consulting and advisory support on an ongoing basis.

CHAPTER 6
3 Steps to Building Your Business Ecosystem

In this chapter, we want to consider where the environment is, that this framework-of generational wealth creation and preservation- exists.

I am going to cover three different segments that align with our user personas of investor, integrator entrepreneur.

The first place where this work occurs, which ties very well to the investor is community.

The second place is ecosystem, which is the integrator's domain.

And thirdly is Virtual Family Office, in relation to the entrepreneur.

Now let us go through these one by one.

For community, there is a saying- an anonymous quote that goes like this: "we are born, we struggle, we build a community, we die".

What that quote tells me essentially, is that -as far as life purpose goes-that building a community is one of the highest achievements *men* can aspire to have, in his or her existence.

In that vein, let us describe what the optimal environments would look like to build, maintain, and exit a business within a community setting, which ensures sustainability.

However, the way we view community today, in society, is either based on a local physical environment, or on identical values.

That is why most of our society lives in silos, where we only associate with those of the same ethnicity or that have the same beliefs or world view as we do.

Our recommendation is that the value system of this post-modern community, be based on a hierarchical framework called PIES.

In ascending order:

P- stands for Physical
I-stands for Intellectual

E-stands for Emotional

S-stands for Spiritual.

Domains of human existence.

The physical domain includes things we can *see*. Classified here as Person-Place-Property. In other words, Body-Environment- and Money.

The intellectual domain refers to how we *think*. This is informed by Education-Experience-Expertise.

The emotional domain is how we *feel*. This governs social contracts and measured as Real-Good-IQ. OR as my young son would call it: Bucket Filler-Bucket Dipper.

What we feel is important because 80% of decisions we make is based on how we feel. We then simply justify our emotional decision with logical explanations.

The spiritual domain identifies what we believe. We all know that belief is one of the strongest forces that you can have, as a human being.

In this framework, spirituality is measured by knowledge, wisdom and understanding.

Where knowledge is the content. Wisdom is the right application of knowledge. And understanding in my opinion is how proven wisdom maps to a variety of use cases, contexts and environments.

So, if we believe something to be true, or if we believe something to be valuable, we have the logical programming to back it up, or we have the feeling to justify it. So, belief is a very strong characteristic. And that is why it is at the top of the hierarchy of PIES.

Now, that is the context and the measures of success, that we would use for qualifying that are members of this community, or performance in general. So those are our hierarchical structures, as opposed to what you have in society, which is based on skin tone, which could be identified as white on top, black on the bottom, Brown and yellow in between.

To be explicit, white refers to Caucasians. Black is Afro descendants. Brown could be Hispanic, Middle Eastern or South Asian. While *yellow* refers to the East and Southeast Asians.

So that is the old form of society, and this is the new.

Now the next point is the ecosystem. This is a unique structure of organizing their business in a functional way that presents a protective moat around it for sustainability.

This relates to the integrator, and you may want to refer to them as subject matter experts. Here we talk about an ecosystem which is more of a functional engine for the community. It is a community of experts, but by role and function.

Here, we put each of these experts into six different buckets. These buckets are Media, Intellectual Property (IP), Product Vendors, Service Vendors, Team, and Distribution.

So, these are the six buckets that form an ecosystem that will support this environment of acquiring, exiting, and integrating the business to create wealth, and to preserve wealth.

The last point is attributable to the entrepreneur, which is for virtual family office. Here is where we begin to explore the context of wealth preservation.

At this point, we are talking about an entrepreneur who is concerned with what we call- owner's equity. A business owner who is considering exiting their business in some way that produces a liquidity event. An event that would provide them financial freedom. And with that financial windfall comes the need for wealth preservation.

Let us say -as an entrepreneur, that we just received this large inflow of cash, from the sale of our business. The next concern is how to ensure that the money does not end up as "easy come, easy go". That it not only lasts through retirement years but also has value left over for our descendants. We are looking for wealth preservation in this scenario.

So, we introduce a concept called the Virtual Family office.

Every entrepreneur that has crossed the *Rubicon* of post wealth creation needs one.

This is where that mechanism of LIFT (law- insurance-finance-tax) comes back into play.

Here it is in the context of wealth preservation.

So, for an entrepreneur who is winding down or having a liquidity event; a person with plans towards sustainable legacy and wealth transfer to future generations; the concept of creating a virtual family office is highly recommended.

This takes care of the financial planning; it takes care of what happens to the tax consequences from selling your business. Before and after.

This takes care of the protection for your estate through trusts and wills and insurance vehicles.

So, there you have it. To recap, we have the community, the ecosystem, and the family office. These are the environments that we recommend for the buying and selling of businesses to occur, for the creation and preservation wealth for these three personas: Investor-Integrator-Entrepreneur.

CHAPTER 7

Profit and Purpose: How to Link Your High-Profit Business to a Greater Purpose

In this chapter, we want to address purpose and fulfillment.

Because let us face it, what is the point of creating and preserving wealth, if we do not feel fulfilled from it all or if there is no purpose to it?

If money is our objective- what happens next after chasing the money?

Take for example the story of Robin Williams who was a beloved comedian and actor that brought joy and laughter to millions of people around the world. However, despite his success and wealth, he struggled with mental health issues and tragically took his own life in 2014. His story serves as a poignant reminder of the importance of purpose and fulfillment in life, and the dangers of pursuing success and wealth without them.

Success and wealth are often seen as the ultimate goals in life, but they are not enough to bring true happiness and fulfillment. While they may provide temporary satisfaction and material comfort, they cannot replace the sense of purpose and meaning that comes from pursuing one's passions and living a life aligned with one's values.

Without a sense of purpose and fulfillment, success and wealth can become empty and meaningless. They can lead to a sense of isolation and disconnection, as one becomes trapped in a cycle of accumulating more and more without ever feeling truly satisfied. This can lead to feelings of depression, anxiety, and even hopelessness, as one realizes that their achievements and possessions cannot fill the void inside.

While success and wealth are certainly desirable, they cannot replace the sense of purpose and fulfillment that comes from living a life aligned with one's passions and values. Without these things, even the most successful and wealthy individuals can find themselves struggling with feelings of emptiness and despair. The lesson we can learn from the life and death of Robin Williams is that true happiness and fulfillment come not from external achievements, but from an internal sense of purpose and meaning.

There is a saying that happiness is directly proportionate to your income, up until about $120K a year- then it starts to decline.

Therefore, the subject of generational wealth creation must have a deeper meaning for there to be a sense of purpose and ultimate fulfillment for the individual.

I am going to propose an idea, that stems from the notion, that the key pillars of any sustainable society would include security, culture, and economics.

We are using the term society loosely, to describe any association of people within a common physical environment, virtual environment, or an organization.

Again, the three key pillars of any sustainable society are fundamentally security, culture, and economics.

So, let us deal with each of these points individually.

For security, this is a basic human need.

According to Maslow's Hierarchy of Needs, safety in terms of food, shelter and clothing are fundamental and will take priority to all other needs and wants.

This is where a person is wanting to feel safe, wanting certainty, and wanting connection.

Because once our basic survival needs are met, as human beings, we tend to want to do more to give life meaning, right?

And we understand that given the opportunity, most people would opt to have social impact on the world if there was a simple roadmap for such a movement.

So, with that notion in mind, the number one key point is security, for the person, physically and emotionally.

All right. So that's security.

The second point is culture.

Culture is what governs our human interactions.

It has to do with a little bit of, adventure, variety, fun, novelty and so on.

How you have fun together is part of your work culture or the culture within a particular demography.

So that is an attribute of culture.

Another attribute is contribution.

How people feel like they can contribute to a community, to their society, is part of the culture of that society.

Culture is one of the most compelling factors that can make or break an organization and affect the rise and fall of a society at large.

In the proceeding chapter when we discuss the makings of a viral movement, you will see how culture plays an important role in that context as well.

Now the third key pillar of society would be economics.

Economics has to do with money. Material things.

Here we want to address the basic human needs for growth and significance.

Defining growth in terms of acceleration or financial growth. And significance in terms of having something substantial, that can be recognized. To be seen, heard and respected.

Economics is another piece of purpose and fulfillment puzzle, that plays into this environment, where we are creating an ecosystem and a sustainable community.

According to Adam Smith in his book-*the wealth of nations* (1881), Economics is described as the allocation of ends and scarce means, which have alternative users.

I like to think that the progression of this in ascending order is, from finance-to- business- to-economics.

Now, the three parameters that we will consider in this category of economics that ties into growth or the three metrics of success in any business context, are: revenue, profits, and equity.

So, the idea that we are proposing for this ecosystem that we are building, as a community, through business acquisition should have these three components, namely: rev share, profit interest and equity participation.

For rev-share, an integrator with a marketable skill should be coming into this ecosystem with the mindset of expecting to share revenues generated with their collaborators.

For profit interest, we recommend profits *only* interest.

This is where someone with an advisory capacity can come into a business and create value that helps the business scale, in exchange for receiving compensation in terms of profit sharing.

So, it is profits only because the tax implication of having equity is a little bit of an inconvenience for such a transient type of engagement.

You can have a contractual agreement where this advisor gets profit only interest in the growth of the company.

And he will get the same treatment as an equity shareholder in the event of an exit.

So, the profit only interest is a way to be compensated for your contribution, without the negative tax implications, on the front end

And on the back end, we will get treatments as a stockholder if the business does sell.

Then the last parameter is equity.

Here you are looking for equity participation in a business venture, whether you are contributing sweat equity or whether you are contributing financial capital.

All of that introduces the conversation around equity.

Which means that ownership is being split amongst individuals.

And this propels the growth and significance of this community, one individual at a time.

Those are the three components security, culture and economics that are put into the context of a person in a particular place and dealing with property. These are the key ingredients for achieving purpose and fulfillment in these environments that we are creating.

CHAPTER 8

Building Your Lasting Legacy in the Acquisition Economy

WHAT IS LEGACY?

As a noun it is an amount of money or property left to someone in a will. For example:

> "my grandmother died and unexpectedly left me a small legacy"

In the US a legacy could be an applicant to a particular college or university who is regarded preferentially because a parent or other relative attended the same institution. For example:

> "being a legacy increased a student's chance of being accepted to a highly selective college by up to 45 percent"

In computing, when we talk of legacy systems, it is denoting or relating to software or hardware that has been superseded but is difficult to replace because of its wide use.

All these definitions of the word legacy are valid and relevant to the discussion in this chapter.

However, when we talk of legacy here, we are simply describing the value of how we want to be remembered.

The impact we want to have on the world.

I like to say, in terms of person, place and property i.e., your body, the environment and your wallet.

Some have always said that *the power of a person's life is* the stories they leave behind.

When a loved one dies, we tend to think about their legacy, about the meaning of their lives.

Thinking of legacy along those lines, I've pulled together seven of my favorite legacy quotes.

FAVORITE QUOTES ABOUT LEGACY

1. Carve your name on hearts, not tombstones. A legacy is etched into the minds of others and the stories they share about you. —*Shannon Alder*

2. The great use of life is to spend it for something that will outlast it. —*William James*

3. Your story is the greatest legacy that you will leave to your friends. It's the longest-lasting legacy you will leave to your heirs. —*Steve Saint*

4. Legacy is not leaving something for people. It's leaving something in people. —*Peter Strople*

5. The greatest legacy one can pass on to one's children and grandchildren is not money or other material things accumulated in one's life, but rather a legacy of character and faith. —*Billy Graham*

6. I glorified you on earth, having accomplished the work that you gave me to do. —*Jesus*

7. Please think about your legacy because you are writing it every day. —*Gary Vaynerchuk*

Despite the way that the lives and legacies of the famous grab our attention, every single one of us leaves a legacy.

Family legacy is not just about what I've created, but about *the story that I'm a part of and share*. In truth, we are always part of bigger narrative.

Our story is never just about ourselves. There have always been events, actions, and people who intersect with our story.

Our challenge is to see the larger narrative, recognizing how others have shaped us and how we impact others.

We influence people every day by what we say and do, by what we write, create and share. And all that influence adds up.

May we use the power of our lives for the lasting good of those we touch, from our own families to our communities and even our online connections.

In the context of wealth creation and wealth preservation, or in terms of generational wealth transfer, this is crucial.

There are three points we want to address, which would be the intergenerational dynamics.

Since we are talking about legacy, about generational wealth creation, generational wealth transfer, generational wealth preservation, it is important to understand the intergenerational relationship dynamics.

What are the components of legacy, what does that look like?

Here we will be talking about generational dynamics within these three categories: baby boomers, the Gen X, and the millennials and younger.

I understand that there are more categories like the Gen Z, and Gen Alpha but for this conversation, which has to do with entrepreneurship, investments, and the working class, we want to keep it to millennials and older.

Without a doubt, in terms of messaging, personalization always helps close deals. Period.

But to take your personalization to the next level, we consider focusing on the individual generational values.

When we say generational values, we do not mean stereotypes.

Instead, we want you to do your homework and find out what resonates with the different generations that make up today's workforce.

Inter-generational relationships refer to the interactions and relationships between individuals from different generations. This can include relationships between grandparents and grandchildren, parents, and children, and even great-grandparents and great-grandchildren. These relationships can have a profound impact on the lives of those involved, and can shape the way that individuals view themselves and their place in the world.

In this chapter, we will explore the dynamics of inter-generational relationships, including the factors that influence them, the benefits and challenges that can arise, and strategies for cultivating healthy and positive relationships between generations.

Factors that Influence Inter-generational Relationships:

There are a number of factors that can influence the dynamics of inter-generational relationships, including cultural norms, family traditions, and individual personalities.

Cultural norms can play a significant role in shaping the expectations and behaviors of different generations.

For example, in some cultures, it is common for younger generations to show respect and deference to their elders, while in others, there may be more of an emphasis on individualism and independence.

Family traditions can also have a powerful impact on inter-generational relationships.

Shared experiences and traditions can help to create a sense of connection and belonging between generations and can provide a framework for understanding and appreciating each other's perspectives and values.

For example, a family that has a tradition of gathering together for holidays or special occasions may find that these shared experiences help to strengthen their relationships and deepen their sense of connection.

Individual personalities can also play a role in shaping inter-generational relationships.

Some individuals may be more naturally inclined to seek out and value the perspectives of others, while others may be more focused on their own experiences and opinions.

Additionally, different generations may have different personality traits that can impact their interactions with each other.

For example, older generations may be more likely to value tradition and stability, while younger generations may be more focused on innovation and change.

Benefits of Inter-generational Relationships:

Inter-generational relationships can offer a number of benefits for individuals and families.

One of the most significant benefits is the opportunity for learning and growth that these relationships provide.

Older generations can offer valuable insights and wisdom based on their life experiences, while younger generations can bring fresh perspectives and new ideas to the table.

By sharing their perspectives and learning from each other, individuals from different generations can gain a deeper understanding of the world around them and develop a broader range of skills and knowledge.

Inter-generational relationships can also help to foster a sense of connection and belonging within families.

By spending time together and sharing experiences, individuals from different generations can develop strong bonds and a sense of shared history and tradition.

This can be particularly important for younger generations, who may be struggling to find their place in the world and establish a sense of identity.

Challenges of Inter-generational Relationships:

While there are many benefits to inter-generational relationships, there can also be challenges that arise.

One of the biggest challenges is the potential for misunderstandings and conflict based on generational differences in values and beliefs.

For example, older generations may hold more traditional views on issues such as gender roles or social norms, while younger generations may be more progressive in their attitudes and beliefs.

These differences can lead to tension and conflict if not handled carefully.

Another challenge of inter-generational relationships is the potential for communication difficulties.

Different generations may have different communication styles and preferences, which can make it difficult to effectively communicate and understand each other.

For example, older generations may prefer more formal or indirect communication, while younger generations may be more casual and direct.

These differences can sometimes lead to misunderstandings or hurt feelings, particularly if one generation feels that the other is not listening or taking their views seriously.

Finally, inter-generational relationships can be impacted by differences in life experience and stage of life. For example, older generations may be retired and have more free time, while younger generations may be focused on building their careers or raising young children. These differences can make it challenging to find time to spend together and to relate to each other's priorities and concerns.

Strategies for Cultivating Positive Inter-generational Relationships:

Despite the challenges that can arise, there are a number of strategies that individuals and families can use to cultivate positive and healthy inter-generational relationships. Some of these strategies include:

1. Respect and empathy: Both younger and older generations can benefit from showing respect and empathy towards each other. This includes listening actively, valuing each other's perspectives and experiences, and being open to learning from each other.

2. Communication: Effective communication is key to building positive relationships between generations. This can include being clear and direct in communication, using active listening skills, and being open to feedback and constructive criticism.

3. Shared experiences: Shared experiences and traditions can help to build a sense of connection and belonging between generations. This can include activities such as family gatherings, holiday celebrations, or even shared hobbies or interests.

4. Education and learning: Encouraging education and learning can help to bridge generational gaps and build understanding and empathy. This can include sharing stories and experiences, reading books or watching films together, or even taking classes or attending workshops together.

5. Flexibility and compromise: Finding ways to be flexible and compromise can help to reduce tension and conflict in inter-generational relationships. This might involve finding ways to accommodate different

schedules or priorities, or being willing to compromise on values or beliefs to find common ground.

Conclusion:

Inter-generational relationships can be complex and challenging, but they can also offer a wealth of benefits for individuals and families. By understanding the factors that influence these relationships, as well as the challenges and opportunities that they present, individuals and families can work to cultivate positive and healthy relationships between generations. By showing respect and empathy, communicating effectively, building shared experiences, encouraging learning and education, and being flexible and willing to compromise, individuals from different generations can work together to create strong and meaningful relationships that enrich their lives and those of future generations.

CHAPTER 9

5 Steps to Move from Legacy to Business Dynasty

What does legacy mean in life?

A legacy is **a lasting impact on the world**. It's a gift that is passed down through generations: money, property or even stories. It can also be a business – or the profits from a business, set up in a foundation or charity. Leaving a legacy means dreaming big and changing the world for the better.

The way most people want to leave a legacy is through a family trust.

A family trust is a wealth management tool that supports the preservation and transference of wealth, beyond a generation.

What is a family trust?

A family trust is a legal arrangement in which property or assets are transferred to a trustee to be managed for the benefit of family members. The trustee has a fiduciary responsibility to manage the trust assets in accordance with the terms of the trust document and for the benefit of the beneficiaries named in the trust.

Creating a family trust can be an effective way to create a legacy by providing for the ongoing financial support and security of family members. Trusts can be designed to provide income to beneficiaries for a set period of time, or even for their entire lifetimes. Additionally, trusts can be set up to allow for the transfer of assets to future generations, which can help ensure that the family's wealth is preserved and passed down for many generations.

One of the key benefits of a family trust is that it can provide significant tax advantages, both during the lifetime of the person creating the trust and after their death. By transferring assets to a trust, the creator of the trust can reduce their estate tax liability and ensure that their assets are distributed in accordance with their wishes.

Overall, a family trust can be an effective tool for creating a legacy by providing ongoing financial support for family members, preserving family wealth and assets, and ensuring that assets are distributed in a manner consistent with the creator's wishes.

The movement to dynasty:

The components of legacy here we are talking about, is to create a movement that inspires positive change in the world and allows like-minded people to participate in a structured and non-disruptive way.

Let me borrow the analogy of an effective movement from the tech industry as suggested by **Stanford's "Technology-enabled Blitzscaling" course.**

They suggest that the progression of an effective movement is Family- Tribe- Village- City- Nation. In that order.

I have adapted this formula to my environment to where Family to me means: Virtual Family Office.

A virtual family office (VFO) **extends access to high-quality wealth management services to a broader range of families.**

Then progressing to the larger community of like-minded folks i.e., Tribe. To me this means: Soul Tribe.

Your soul tribe, or soul family, is **a group of people who you intuitively connect with on a deep level**. Soul tribe relationships are anything but shallow. There's a deep resonance at a soul level that you intuitively understand is different and special. Shout out to *Vision 2020*.

And then the wealth creation happens at the outer level, which could be considered the village or the community, where, you know, wealth creation or wealth preservation happens, as we described in the previous chapter.

And then, for dynasty, our philosophy is the equitable distribution of wealth and resources.

WHAT IS A DYNASTY?

Dynasty is a succession of rulers of the same line of descent.

Like the Qing dynasty that ruled China for nearly 300 years.

Or a powerful group or family that maintains its position for a considerable time born into a powerful political dynasty, a baseball dynasty.

For our environment, each member is royalty, and run their private empires in connection and contribution to the larger economy.

This means that the operation is sustainable because of ongoing reciprocity. Where everyone, pulls their weight and contributes their fair share to the collective.

That way, everything is in balance- including debt and reward; sentiment and logic; gender and responsibility.

There is a quote here from scripture that says : he who does not work, let him not eat. (, 2 Thessalonians 3:10)

Everyone is basically contributing what they can to creating this ecosystem that is self sustaining. And you know, the breakdown of all the functions.

So, what people can contribute are acquisitions, methodology, and delivery.

Acquisitions could be business acquisition or client acquisition.

Methodology largely has to do with people that have intellectual property, or proprietary systems.

Delivery is the hands-on deck, those that do the actual implementation, and those that provide client support.

And the definition that we have for dynasty is basically linked to the financial term called royalties.

According to Tony Robbins, the six human needs are Certainty, Uncertainty, Contribution, Connection, Growth and Significance.

Certainty is the need to feel safe. To be assured that there is a proven system that guarantees the expected outcome to a high probability.

Uncertainty refers to variety. Adventure. Magic.

The need for people to have fun with their work and a lifestyle filled with play.

Connection relates to empathy and matters of the heart. People want to feel seen, heard and understood. They want to be aligned with like minds with similar values. The want to belong to a community and be engaged.

Growth is the key to happiness. When we are not growing, we feel stagnated, bored, and even depressed. Growth in business and other areas of your personal life is essential to obtain the satisfaction that comes with a sense of accomplishment.

Significance produces respect. It means having impact in the world or a positive effect on the lives of people. Significance has to do with pride. Not arrogance but something of great importance that we can be proud of.

For example, it is significant to be the first millionaire in your family. Or the first university graduate.

Other things that could be significant are: a good name, title and position, accolades, wealth and fortune.

I particularly like the genre of monarchy as a ruling structure. The idea that the culture and personality of a people is influenced by one person or one family.

The simplicity of the decision making that comes with that much power resting in one person.

This ties back to the idea of *royalties* in our model (pun intended) and the fulfillment of the need for significance.

Therefore, we offer that the members of our community would view themselves through the lens of royalty as we build up each business ecosystem to into their empire.

Like we described in the last chapter, we have broken down financial compensation into revenues, in terms of rev share, profits in terms of profit-only-interest and equity in terms of equity participation.

In this dynamic, when people come into this ecosystem, looking to engage with business acquisition, or accelerating the business through integration, they should be looking at compensation by way of either revenue, profits, or equity.

When you are set up to generate recurring income over time, this is what we are classifying as royalties.

The more perpetual in nature, the longer in nature, the more like a in traditional royalty, it is.

So, to recap: we are creating a society, a community, a system that allows people to create and preserve wealth that can last them generations. And that is akin to a dynasty where people are dignified, regal and earn royalties.

CHAPTER 10

Living the Dream

Living the dream means that **someone is living his best life; that he is achieving the goals he wants to achieve; that he has all the material comforts and/or relationships that he wants to have.**

A good friend of mine talks about not just leaving a legacy but <u>living</u> a legacy.

On the concept of living the dream, we want to talk about the bigger, brighter future, after we've considered all that can go into acquisition entrepreneurship, to create generational wealth, and to build a legacy and to impact the world in some positive and everlasting way.

Now those are very high-minded objectives.

Even below that, we look at personal objectives. Not everyone has the same happily ever after. Some of us want to own a private island. Others want to fly around in private jets.

Many others want to have the time and money freedom to travel around the world and live in different countries and be a *digital nomad.*

But to arrive at the immediate dream of the average entrepreneur, investor, and integrator, I will rely on the pain points that we want to relieve.

This is what it looks like for each of the unique avatars.

For an investor, which is someone who has essentially access to capital, and an appetite to take the risk, to acquire a business in order to expand it and start to create profitable assets. This person essentially wants to become a business owner. That is their happily ever after.

They want to own the business and not have to work in it.

To have operators that can run the day to day while they do some strategic activities.

They exist above the business. So that, at a high level is what the investor wants.

The integrator wants to essentially become an investor.

To invest with mostly sweat equity.

They want to have some skin in the game.

They want to have some equity participation.

They work ON the business, to accelerate it.

The entrepreneur wants to essentially exit his day-to-day responsibilities.

He wants to still be a part of the growth of the company. So would rather exit and become a consultant where they don't have to worry about the day to day but focus on the areas that they enjoy doing. Maybe that's the creative aspect.

So, they're working IN the business in that regard. Or as a manager of some sort, where they're just getting a salary, and they don't have to think about the liability of business ownership.

What is noteworthy is that these three distinct individuals all merged into the same person eventually. Yet at different stages, they have different needs.

Now, how do we help you accomplish these dreams?

For the investor, what we're helping you do is to get you access to capital. To get you deal flow, and to find your motivated sellers who want your contribution to their plans for an exit or for an expansion.

For the integrator, we want to find you deals to work on. To find you paying gigs.

People that will bring you on to accelerate their businesses once they found an investor or they have an investment to make for the integration and acceleration of their business.

For the entrepreneur, what they're looking for is investment capital, and human capital.

Basically, if somebody came along with an established ecosystem that says, you know, we can deal with everything else, you just do the part that you love, (which could just be potentially, let's say, writing copy or just client facing or any small part of the business that you want to be involved in) and we will take care of the rest.

What does that look like? So, these are the three instances, where we can contribute to getting you your, bigger, better future.

Now, if we're talking about these avatars in the early stages, the origin stories may look a little different.

For the investor, you may be looking at a professional who is trying to transition from being, for example, a company executive, to becoming a *wantrapreneur* and to ultimate graduate to becoming an investor.

That's a long journey for that person, right.

And what they're looking for is time freedom. What they're looking for is to exit the rat race. What they're looking for is to have control of something- like control of their destiny, control of their schedule, and finances.

To avoid the depression of being obligated to be doing one thing, when you would rather be doing something else.

These are the pain points that we are looking to relieve in that situation.

And for all the technical consultants, like an engineer, for instance, that is looking forward to retirement, but doesn't know what that looks like, we could be talking to them about potentially becoming a *train the trainer* situation.

Here they can exit the doing and become more of a guide and mentor, a trainer.

They can pass down that knowledge that they've accumulated over those 20, 30,40-year careers, to the new generation.

To modernize it that way, while you still have an impact.

While you remain active and relevant to your industry.

While exiting the aspects that are becoming redundant.

For the entrepreneur, who is a solopreneur for example, this offer is even more compelling.

If you come in to say, you know, it will be hard to exit your business as a solopreneur because what are we buying?

You are the most valued asset in your company, and we can't just buy you, can we?

You are the business. And we all know that the more the business relies on you the less valuable it is.

So, how do we increase that business value and give you the opportunity to potentially exit at the highest valuation, while having something to transfer to a new owner.

This is where we can come in. To build an ecosystem around what you do. To put in processes, like standard operating procedures (SOPs). To package your intellectual property (IP). To solidify the supply chain, and to have a strong lead generation system.

Also to put in place all the vendors that supply you either service or products and to formalize your structure for teams and resources.

So, all these things need to be in place, so, that your core business becomes more valuable. Because now it has, a moat around it.

These are values that we create that will give these individuals the kind of life that they can be proud of while they're building their legacy.

To say you're not likely sailing off into the sunset is because most people like to stay engaged and active and still working.

But now you're working with passion, right?

You have the right structure that is aligned with your values.

Now, that's living the dream.

CONCLUSION

I just have one question for you... will you be a part of the new wave of wealth, or will you sit on the sidelines and watch it pass you by?

One of the fastest ways (maybe *the* fastest way) to build wealth is to acquire a business and improve it.

As an investor, if you can find the right motivated seller and the right deal, you could end up with a cash flowing business as an asset.

The key to a successful dealmaking, is to have the right set of professionals around you, to guide you through the process of buying the business, and beyond.

You need LIFT- Law, Insurance, Finance and Tax.

For the entrepreneur looking to sell their business at some future date, for the best value possible, it is important to take certain proactive actions because selling a business is not easy.

In fact, according to the International Business Brokers Association (IBBA), up to 90% of businesses listed for sale, do not sell.

If you are thinking of selling your company in the next 3-7years, and you do not want to become one of the 90%, you will be best served to retain an M&A advisor, (not a broker).

While both M&A advisors and business brokers are professionals who can assist in the sale of a business, there are some key differences between the two that might make an M&A advisor a better choice in certain situations.

M&A advisors typically work with larger, more complex transactions than business brokers, and are often better equipped to handle the complexities of these transactions. M&A advisors are typically more experienced in negotiating and structuring deals and may have a larger network of contacts in the industry, allowing them to identify potential buyers more quickly and efficiently.

In addition, M&A advisors often provide a higher level of personalized service and attention to detail than business brokers, which can be important in complex transactions where attention to detail is critical. M&A advisors also typically have a more comprehensive understanding of the market and industry trends, which can help ensure that the transaction is structured in a way that maximizes value for the seller.

Overall, while business brokers can be a good choice for smaller, less complex transactions, M&A advisors are often a better choice for larger, more complex transactions where a higher level of expertise and personalized service is required.

Therefore, the M&A Advisor or Consultant is an intermediary which in our model we call an integrator.

When you are an integrator with so much to offer, in terms of business acceleration and operations, it is important to understand how to convert your skills to assets, and assets to wealth.

The way to do that is called Consulting-For-Equity (CFE). This is where you shift your mindset from *not only earning a paycheck* but also earning a piece of the business as compensation for your contributions.

The first thing to do is to make a list of all your super-powers. This is a list of all your tangible and intangible skills.

Then list out the typical problems that you use your skills to solve for your clients. Call them the biggest common pain points (BCCP), of your ideal clients.

Now evaluate the impact your solution provides to your client. Use this as a measure of ROI (return on investment). For example, if you were paid ten thousand dollars to deploy a marketing campaign for a small business, and they generated one hundred thousand dollars in sales from that campaign, that is equal to ten times the return on their investment through you.

If you can leverage that information in your next fee negotiation, to include either a revenue sharing payment structure, or an equity kicker, you will be in good shape in the long run.

As we embark on this journey of wealth creation through business acquisitions, we must pause to consider what the optimal future state of our lives would be.

We know the three most important aspects of our lives are health, relationships, and wealth.

According to the scriptures: *Money answereth all things*. So, we are proposing that taking care of the wealth aspect would be helpful for your relationships and health as well.

When we think about the meaning of life and such existential questions, it is important to note what we might consider a common thread amongst all human beings- regardless of politics, beliefs, or cultural background.

Tony Robbins talks about six common human needs namely: the need for Growth, the need for Connection, the need for Significance, the need for Certainty, the need for Uncertainty or Variety, and the need for Contribution.

Using these as a reference point, it is easy to imagine that one would gain growth, connection, contribution, certainty, uncertainty, and significance, through the process of business acquisitions, especially when conducted within the context of a community setting.

Now, the biggest risk we face after learning all these concepts, is to do nothing.

Granted, that the business acquisition journey or any entrepreneurship journey for that matter, is not for the faint of heart.

However, with some self motivation and proper planning, and professional support, success is inevitable.

The key is to want it.

Many people wish to have wealth, but very few truly want it.

Wanting it implies planning for it. Taking massive action and doing the work. Accepting the changes, it will produce in your life.

A good exercise for mindset, is to think about what you might do with more money, more time. How would you create more magic in your life?

If the images you visualize give you the feeling of freedom, joy and abundance, then you must seriously consider the course of action that this book is suggesting.

The risks of not acting include financial hardship, interpersonal difficulties when you work with the wrong people, and or lack of fulfillment when executed within a narrow life context.

It's your move now.

What will you do?

AUTHOR BIOGRAPHY

Afam Elue is an aspiring Social Psychologist with a diverse professional and cultural background.

Born in West Africa, he began his career in Corporate Banking with what is now Africa's largest bank.

He moved to the US in 2004 for post graduate studies, earning an MBA (master's in business administration) degree from the University of Dallas in Texas.

He continued his work in financial services with companies like Citi Financial and Edward Jones Investments before transitioning to IT project management.

Today he is an Investor, Business Consultant and Tech Entrepreneur. As a Microsoft Partner, he specializes in acquiring and rolling up other IT firms in order to scale quickly.

He lives in Toronto Canada with his wife -Elaine, a Singaporean National, and their three children Chino, Kanayo and Tobe.

In 2021, he was a candidate for the Green Party in the Federal Elections in Canada contesting to be a Member of Parliament on the platform of Climate Action in response to the global climate emergency.

He is the Founder and Chairperson of ABC (African Business Community), a Not-For-Profit, social enterprise focused on helping entrepreneurs of afro-descent towards the creation and preservation of wealth.